THE NEW
CREEPY CRAWLY
COLLECTION

GRASSHOPPERS

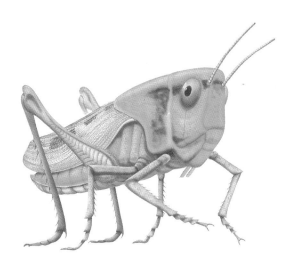

For a free color catalog describing Gareth Stevens' list of high-quality books and multimedia programs, call 1-800-542-2595 (USA) or 1-800-461-9120 (Canada). Gareth Stevens Publishing's Fax: (414) 225-0377. See our catalog, too, on the World Wide Web: http://gsinc.com

Library of Congress Cataloging-in-Publication Data

Coleman, Graham, 1963-
    Grasshoppers / by Graham Coleman ; illustrated by Tony Gibbons.
      p. cm. -- (The New creepy crawly collection)
    Includes bibliographical references and index.
    Summary: Examines the anatomy, behavior, varied habitats, life cycle, enemies, and different kinds of grasshoppers.
    ISBN 0-8368-1915-2 (lib. bdg.)
    1. Grasshoppers--Juvenile literature. 2. Katydids--Juvenile literature.
[1. Grasshoppers.] I. Gibbons, Tony, ill. II. Title. III. Series.
QL508.A2C65 1997
595.7'26--dc21   97-7334

This North American edition first published in 1997 by
Gareth Stevens Publishing
1555 North RiverCenter Drive, Suite 201
Milwaukee, Wisconsin 53212 USA

This U.S. edition © 1997 by Gareth Stevens, Inc. Created with original © 1996 by Quartz Editorial Services, 112 Station Road, Edgware HA8 7AQ U.K.

Additional illustrations by Clare Heronneau.

Consultant: Matthew Robertson, Senior Keeper, Bristol Zoo, Bristol, England.

Printed in Mexico

1 2 3 4 5 6 7 8 9 01 00 99 98 97

THE NEW
CREEPY CRAWLY
COLLECTION

GRASSHOPPERS

by Graham Coleman
Illustrated by Tony Gibbons

Gareth Stevens Publishing
MILWAUKEE

Contents

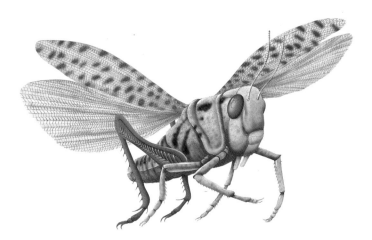

Getting to know
grasshoppers

City-dwellers will rarely see them. But most people who live in the countryside are probably familiar with grasshoppers, even though these small insects are often hard to spot.

You'll also find out how they mate, how they "sing," what they eat, and the answers to the following questions: Do they have any enemies? Could you keep one as a pet? Are there any grasshoppers that can be dangerous to us?

Keep reading and become a grasshopper expert in your own right!

In fact, you are much more likely to *hear* grasshoppers than see them.

As you will discover in the next few pages of this book, many different types of grasshoppers live on our planet.

Great jumpers

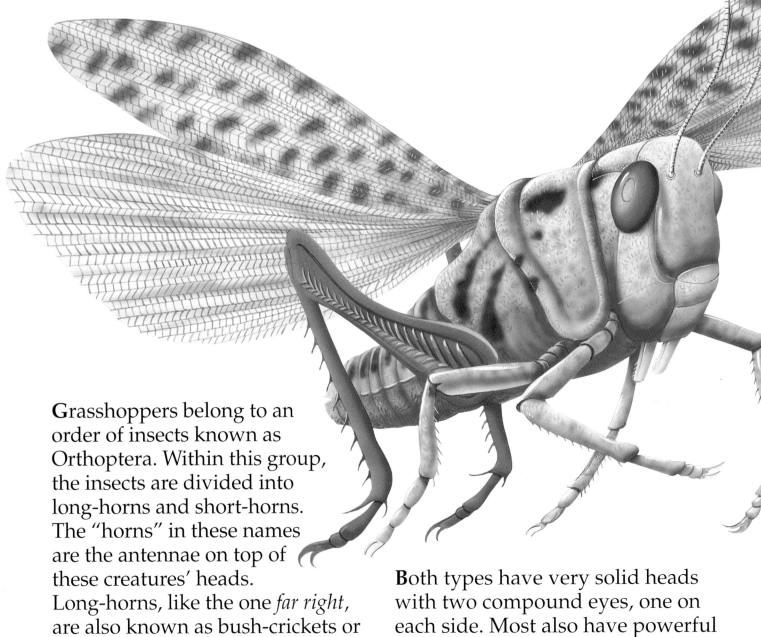

Grasshoppers belong to an order of insects known as Orthoptera. Within this group, the insects are divided into long-horns and short-horns. The "horns" in these names are the antennae on top of these creatures' heads. Long-horns, like the one *far right*, are also known as bush-crickets or katydids; while short-horns, like the one *above*, are *true* grasshoppers.

Both types have very solid heads with two compound eyes, one on each side. Most also have powerful jaws for cutting cleanly through their plant food.

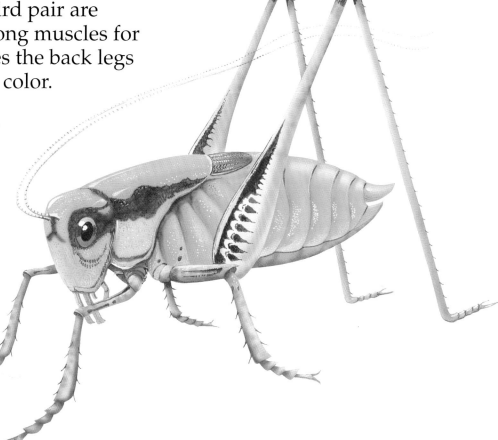

They have two antennae on their heads. The antennae on the short-horns, as their name suggests, are shorter and thicker than those of the long-horns (katydids). The antennae are delicate sense organs, used for feeling, and look a little like radio antennae.

Grasshoppers have three pairs of legs. The first two pairs are for walking, but the third pair are larger and have strong muscles for jumping. Sometimes the back legs are even a different color.

Most grasshoppers have two pairs of wings. Only one pair is used for flying. The other pair provides an extra protective layer when the grasshopper is simply resting or hopping around.

The outer pair of wings also carries special sound equipment for the grasshopper's "song." But most grasshoppers do not spend a lot of time in the air. Some types do not even have wings at all or have just poorly-developed ones.

Grasshoppers can vary in size. The European long-nosed species, for example, is about 2.5 inches (6 centimeters) long. But one South American grasshopper measures 6 inches (15 cm) in length.

7

Musical

If you have ever walked through a field alive with an unusual chirping sound, chances are that it was being made not by a bird but by male grasshoppers.

To make their "song," most male grasshoppers rub part of their legs against the thickest veins on their outer wings, in much the same way that a violinist moves the bow over the strings of a violin. This process is called "stridulation." Each type of grasshopper makes a slightly different sound. Many experts can even identify a specific type of grasshopper just by listening to the sound it makes.

The faster a male grasshopper rubs its legs against its wings, the higher the sound will be. And grasshoppers making slow strokes will produce just a low hum.

Grasshoppers sing for several reasons. One of the most important is to attract the attention of a female.

bugs

Scientists have played back recordings of a male grasshopper's song to a female. The females of one type of grasshopper also "sing." But they do not sing to attract a mate. Instead, their songs are probably made to scare enemies away.

Male katydids (the long-horn grasshoppers) make their songs in another way, by rubbing the tops of their wings together. They have their ears hidden away in tiny slits in their legs, not on the sides of the head, like humans.

If you ever get a chance to observe a katydid up close, you may notice that it sometimes swings its legs back and forth. If it does so, it is probably a female listening for a male's song.

Other types of grasshoppers, meanwhile, have their hearing organs on the last part of the thorax, or even on their abdomen.

What's on the menu?

True grasshoppers are entirely vegetarian. As herbivores, they never eat other animals, only plants. The main item on their menu is the grass that surrounds them. They also eat leaves and flowers and even nibble on pieces of fruit.

Katydids, however, enjoy a diet different from the *true* grasshoppers. The oak bush-cricket, for example, on the *left* of this picture, does not just eat plants. It likes grass, but it will also hunt, kill, and eat centipedes and small insects such as greenflies.

Katydids will even resort to cannibalism — eating members of their own species — if they do not have enough food to eat or enough space in which to live.

Varied

Grasshoppers usually live on or just above the ground in grassy or leafy areas, just as their name suggests. They are active during the day, "singing" by rubbing their legs against their wings, and feeding on the abundant vegetation that surrounds them. The grasshopper's habitat does not always have to be lush and fertile, however. Many grasshoppers can live in deserts or muddy areas — as long as there are some patches of grass around, as you can see in the illustration *below*. But the long-horned grasshoppers, also known

habitats

as katydids, such as the one *below,* live mostly in trees and bushes, although some may also live on the ground. Because their back legs are not as strong as those of the *true* grasshopper, katydids usually live at a higher level, where they will not need to jump around as much. If you are looking for them, remember that the long-horned grasshoppers (katydids) prefer the afternoons and evenings. And some will only come out at night, when their "songs" sound even louder because it is quiet all around them.

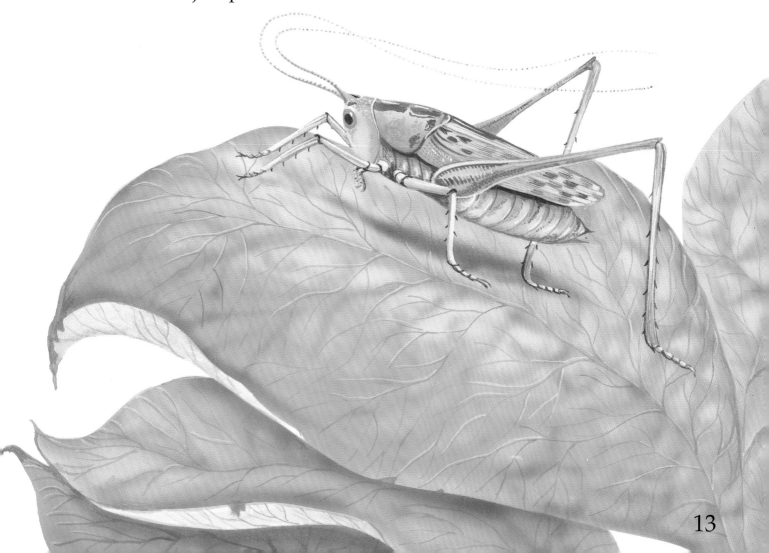

Many types of grasshoppers have colors that blend in with their environment. This way, they can hide within their habitat and stay safe from predators.

Those that live in the desert, for example, tend to be sand-colored. Those that live in tropical areas tend to be the same color as grass. These colors provide camouflage for the insects.

hide-and-seek

It is not always possible, even for an entomologist, to identify a specific type of grasshopper just by its color. Some grasshoppers within the same species may sometimes be a different shade of the same color or have varying body patterns, such as spots or stripes.

One type of North African bush-cricket, or katydid, can even disguise itself as an ant. This is a useful trick in areas where whole armies of ants can attack grasshoppers. Another South African species looks more like a stone than an actual grasshopper. This makes it very hard to spot.

As long as a grasshopper keeps still and blends in with its surroundings, it may look like a blade of grass, a leaf, or a twig, and its enemies will not recognize it. But if it *is* accidentally disturbed, a grasshopper can spring into action rapidly by using its powerful back legs to leap away from danger. You can see one doing just that in this illustration. Other grass-hoppers nearby would probably soon do the same.

Birth of a

Soon after mating, a female grasshopper lays between 30 and 100 eggs, releasing them into the ground in a special covering called an egg-pod. She may lay up to ten batches of eggs at a time.

Just figure it out! This makes it possible for her to produce one thousand babies.

To make sure the pods are buried deeply enough, the female inflates her abdomen, making it four times the size it would be normally. This means she can dig very deep holes.

Between two and four weeks later, the eggs hatch. The tiny creatures emerging are known as nymphs.

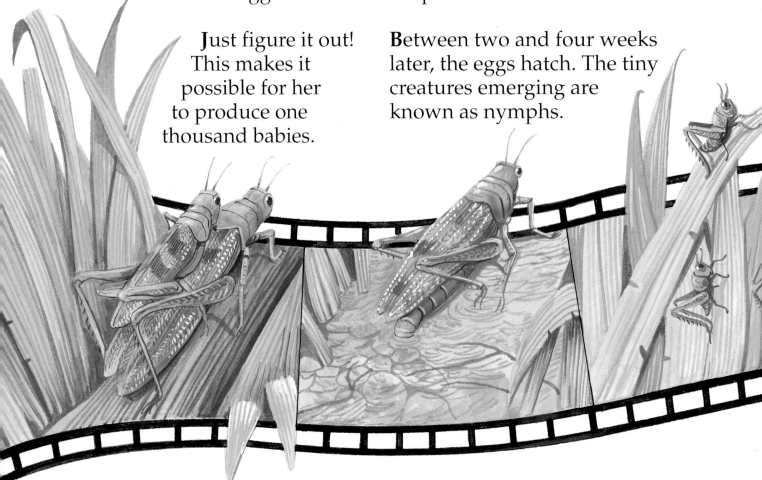

The grasshopper buries the pods by pushing them with her abdomen.

As you can see, they are very unusual-looking at this stage.

grasshopper

The nymphs now start to shed their skin. This process is called molting. In all, the young grasshoppers will molt between five and eight more times, gradually getting bigger as their wings develop. They are not very colorful at this stage.

It will now hang on a twig or some other convenient resting place and let its wings dry. What a beautiful creature it is!

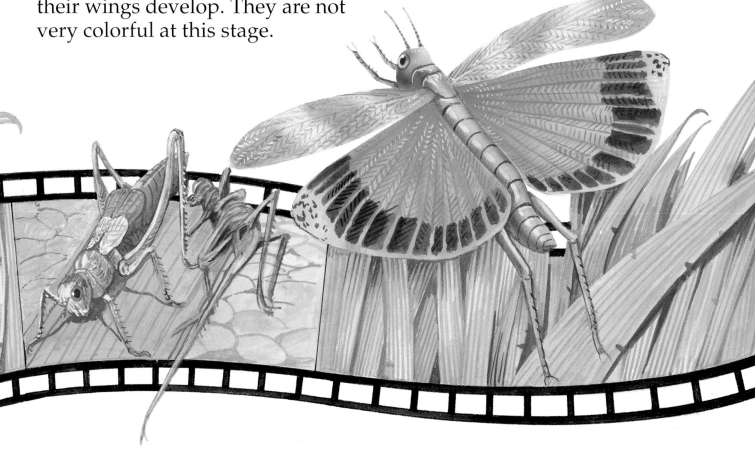

Then, at last, the day comes for the grasshopper to shed its skin for the final time.

Soon it will make its first flight. And within a few weeks, it will be ready to produce a new generation.

The dreaded locust

No one needs to be afraid of an ordinary grasshopper. After all, it will not attack or bite. Instead, it spends most of its time simply eating, resting, and "singing."

But certain large grasshoppers are different. They can swarm in enormous numbers and cause terrible devastation to crops. These dreaded insects are the locusts.

Usually, locusts live on their own. But if conditions are right and food is plentiful, they start to breed rapidly. Millions of nymphs gather in huge groups and march off together, eating any plant in their path. When they develop wings, they fly off in huge swarms.

These fearful insects are usually found only in warm regions of the world. They have enormous appetites and will eat all sorts of available vegetation, including cultivated crops. Famine may then be a result.

Many regions of Africa, America, Australia, and Asia have suffered from devastation by locusts. Total costs that are the result of destroyed crops and the loss of food supplies for humans and other animals can be enormous.

Other jumping

Grasshoppers are not the only small creatures that would do extremely well for their size in high-jump events, if such competitions existed. Let's meet some of the others. Springtails, which are tiny and have the scientific name of Collembola, have no wings and live mainly under stones, in soil, or on the surface of water. If disturbed, the springtail, *below*, can use its tail to catapult itself forcefully into the air. What a spectacular leap!

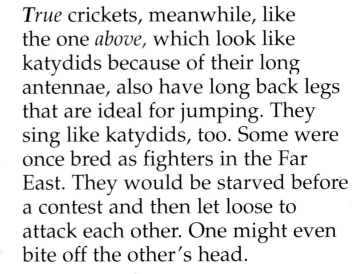

True crickets, meanwhile, like the one *above*, which look like katydids because of their long antennae, also have long back legs that are ideal for jumping. They sing like katydids, too. Some were once bred as fighters in the Far East. They would be starved before a contest and then let loose to attack each other. One might even bite off the other's head.

insects

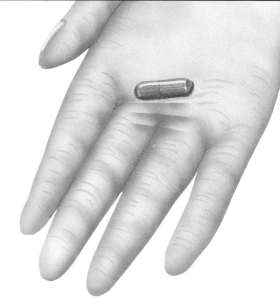

If you ever come across a click beetle that has somehow landed upside-down, watch it closely for a while. At first, it will probably stay still, pretending to be dead so that you won't harm it. Then, suddenly, the click beetle may fling itself into the air. This is the beetle's way of trying to get right-side up, as shown in the illustration *below.* Listen carefully as it does this, because chances are you will hear it go "click." This is, of course, how it got its name.

You may even have a jumping insect of your own. "Magical" jumping beans, often sold as small toys and shown *above,* are not really magical at all. Inside each pill-like container is a seed. In this seed is a moth caterpillar. It feeds contentedly off the inside of the seed, but hates heat. So it "jumps" along as it searches for shade. Be warned, though. If you make a jumping bean jump too much, it can die from exhaustion.

Did you know?

How many species of grasshoppers are there?

There are thousands of species worldwide. Some have fascinating names — the great green grasshopper of England; the great shielded grasshopper of New Guinea; and the giant painted grasshopper of the Galápagos Islands.

Is it true that locusts are mentioned in the Bible?

Thousands of years ago, so the *Old Testament* tells us, the children of Israel were slaves in Egypt. Moses, their leader, was trying to get the Egyptian king, known as the Pharaoh, to set them free. Ten plagues were sent by God to try and soften the Pharaoh's heart. The plagues included darkness, frogs, water turned to blood, flies, boils, hail, a cattle disease, death of the Egyptian firstborn . . . and locusts.

▼ *How do some grasshoppers protect themselves from predators?*

Most grasshoppers are well camouflaged and can remain hidden from enemies for most of the time. But some can also give off a bad-smelling substance. If alarmed, they will produce this nasty fluid to warn predators that they will *not* make a tasty meal, as you can see in the illustration *below*.

What methods can be used to stop locusts that cause devastation?

It has sometimes been so critical to get rid of locust swarms that people have tried anything they could think of to get rid of them as quickly as possible. In some parts of the world, people have tried to drive huge swarms of locusts into the sea using sticks. Others have made dreadful noises with tin cans in an attempt to frighten the locusts away. Sometimes, too, smoke screens and flames have been used. Chemical methods, including the use of poisons, have worked, but there is always a great danger that the chemical poisons will kill harmless creatures in addition to the pesky locusts. Insects that are natural predators of locusts have also been used at times.

How large is a swarm of locusts?

Swarms have been reported that extend to as much as 150 miles (242 kilometers) long and over 10 miles (17 km) wide — or possibly even bigger. Just imagine the damage all those locusts could cause and how dark they would make the sky! Even during the daytime, it would seem like night.

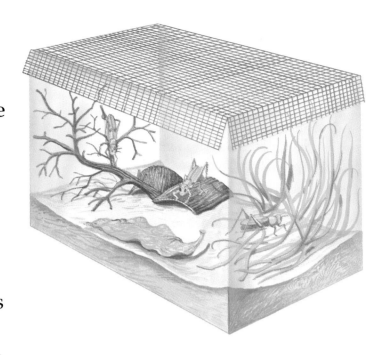

▲ Can you keep a grasshopper as a pet?

If you would like to study a grasshopper for a while, you may be able to catch one with a butterfly net. Be gentle with the grasshopper. Have a large glass container ready. The container's cover should have holes in it so the grasshopper will be able to breathe. Give it some fresh grass and leaves, and maybe a twig to climb. Return the grasshopper to its natural environment when you have finished looking at it. Don't keep it in the container for too long. Grasshoppers prefer being outside, and yours might want to look for a mate.

Glossary

abdomen — the part of a grasshopper's body that is located behind the thorax and which contains the stomach.

camouflage — markings or coloring that help organisms blend in with their natural background.

entomologist — a scientist who studies insects.

famine — a state of starvation caused by a lack of food.

habitat — the natural surroundings or environment of a plant or animal.

herbivores — plant-eating animals.

nymph — the larva of a grasshopper after it has hatched from its egg and before it turns into an adult.

species — a group of plants or animals that share similar physical characteristics.

stridulation — the process of rubbing the legs against the wings to produce a "singing" sound.

thorax — the chest cavity, which houses the heart, is also known as the thorax.

vegetarian — eating only plant foods, or a diet of vegetables, fruits, nuts, grain, and sometimes eggs or dairy products.

Books and Videos

Flying Insects. WINGS series. Patricia Lantier-Sampon (Gareth Stevens)

Grasshopper. June Loves (SRA Scholastic Group)

Grasshoppers. Lynn M. Stowe (Rourke Corporation)

Grasshoppers and Crickets. Barrie Watts (Watts)

Grasshoppers. (Films for the Humanities and Sciences)

Insects Galore. (Journal Films and Video)

Index